99 GAMES FOR CUB SCOUTS

BY

A. DAVIES

Illustrations by Peter Harrison

GLASGOW
BROWN, SON & FERGUSON, LTD., Scout Publishers
4-10 DARNLEY STREET

First Edition	–	1975
Revised	–	–	1977
Reprinted	–	–	1980
Reprinted	–	–	1983
Reprinted	–	–	1985

ISBN 0 85174 304 8

(ISBN 0 85174 215 7 First Edition)

© 1985 Brown, Son & Ferguson, Ltd., Glasgow G41 2SD

Made and Printed in Great Britain

CONTENTS

99 Games for Cub Scouts

(1) SNEAKY SIMON.

EQUIPMENT REQUIRED—A blindfold, a length of cloth or rope about one third of a metre (1 foot) long.

The Cub Scouts form a large circle holding hands. A Cub Scout Leader stands inside the circle blindfolded, having a strip of cloth or short length of rope tucked into the back of his belt. Akela chooses a Cub Scout, who has to creep up to the blindfolded Leader and snatch the cloth. The Cub Scout Leader tries to capture the Cub Scout.

(2) PILE 'EM ON.

EQUIPMENT REQUIRED—None other than the various articles found around the room.

The Sixes take up position in the four corners of the room. Each Six selects one Cub Scout who is to act as the 'aeroplane' in the game. At the word 'Go' the rest of the Six gather pieces of equipment and pile, hang or balance them on their aeroplane. This continues until the word 'Freeze' is given, when everyone stands still. Then at the further command 'Fly', the four aeroplanes move into the centre of the room attempting to keep their loads intact. In the centre Cub Scout Leaders count the separate number of articles in each load. The winning Six have the highest number.

(3) IMPEDE.

EQUIPMENT REQUIRED—None.

All but two of the Cub Scouts line up along one wall of the room facing the centre. In the centre of the room, holding hands are the two Cub Scouts. When these two are ready they shout 'Go' and the rest are given a time limit by Akela to reach the safety of the opposite wall. The two Cub Scouts holding hands attempt to impede the others, delaying them in such a way that they are still in the act of crossing when the time limit expires. They are then considered captured and must join hands with those already in the centre. When a full chain extends right across the room a further rank is begun in front of the first one, the only difference being that this line has its back turned towards the remaining uncaptured Cub Scouts. The last one captured is the winner.

(4) CHUNNELL.

EQUIPMENT REQUIRED—None.

This game is best played by two teams, but can be played by four. The teams line up in Indian file equidistant from a Cub Scout Leader who has both arms outstretched towards the teams. At the word 'Go' the Cub Scouts jump legs astride with the exception of the back member of each team. He crawls through the tunnel formed by the legs of his team and as soon as he appears between the legs of the front member of the team, he hauls him to his feet. The movement is continuous for as soon as the back boy passes under the legs of those in front of him, the new back boy may immediately follow and so on. Moving in this way the team will approach the Cub Scout Leader, the first to touch his outstretched hand is the winner.

(5) BOMB THE BRIDGE.

EQUIPMENT REQUIRED—One plastic football.

Each Cub Scout chooses a position on the floor and stands feet astride. The selected spot must be away from the wall. One Cub Scout is given a plastic football and he must attempt to either throw it between some other Cub Scout's legs or throw it to hit someone below the knees. The other Cub Scouts can defend their legs and the gap between with their hands and arms. A Cub Scout must sit down if; (a) He overbalances, (b) He moves his feet, (c) Is hit below the knees with the ball or the ball passes between his legs. The last one remaining standing is the winner. Those Cub Scouts sat down may still participate in the game by intercepting the ball and throwing it at the boys still standing. Those standing may, of course, intercept the ball themselves by catching it.

(6) STOW THE CARGO.

EQUIPMENT REQUIRED—Two large cardboard boxes or equivalent containers. At least twenty beanbags or some other similar article, for example rolled paper balls secured by sticky tape.

The room is divided as in the diagram. The Cub Scouts are

divided into two teams 'A' and 'B'. Team 'A's box is placed in position 'A 1' and similarly team 'B's box is placed in area 'B 1'. All of team 'A' with the exception of one chosen Cub Scout then take up position in area 'A 2', the other Cub Scout takes up position by his team's box. The team is armed with half of the beanbags. Similarly team 'B' is given the other half of the beanbags and it takes up position in area 'B2' with one member of their team guarding their box.

At the command 'Go' each team attempts to toss their beanbags across the other team and into their own box. Each beanbag that is successfully thrown is left in the box and counted up to determine the winner as soon as Akela calls 'Freeze'. As the beanbags cross the opponents' area they may be intercepted and then redirected. If the beanbag misses the box, the team member in the box area may return the beanbag to his own team. Once again these passes may be intercepted. Akela may either set a time limit or wait until all the beanbags are in one or other of the boxes.

(7) OBSTACLE COURSE.

EQUIPMENT REQUIRED—Various things such as chairs, lashing ropes, balls, etc.

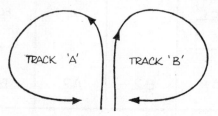

TRACK 'A'   TRACK 'B'

The course is best laid out in a double circle as shown in the diagram. The Cub Scouts are divided into two teams, one following one track around the course, the other team following the other. It is important to make sure that each team encounters exactly the same obstacles on their circuit of the course as the other. Here are some examples of simple obstacles and tasks that can be included. (*a*) Skip ten times. (*b*) Crawl through a tunnel of chairs. (*c*) Spin round three times. (*d*) Throw up and catch a ball four times, and so on. The game is run as a relay.

(8) TAGGED.

EQUIPMENT REQUIRED—One roll of sellotape.

One Six leaves the room and the remaining Sixes take up positions within the room in any place they can conceive of where they consider that they will be safe from attack from the other Six. Each member of the Six outside the room is given two small pieces of sticky sellotape. The lights within the room are turned off and the attacking Six must locate the others in the dark and attempt to tag them by sticking a piece of sellotape on to them. If a Cub Scout becomes aware that he has been tagged, he may attempt to locate and remove the tag. However, once the lights are turned on by Akela everyone must freeze and no more tags may be removed. An inspection is made by the Cub Scout Leaders for tags and a score is made, then the roles are changed round. Any Cub Scout failing to freeze when the lights are put on is counted as tagged by the Cub Scout Leader scoring.

(9) IT'S ONLY SAFE ON....

EQUIPMENT REQUIRED—None.

Two Cub Scouts are detailed as catchers and take up position in the centre of the room. Akela then says, 'It's only safe on . . . .' and then proceeds to name something such as 'red' or 'metal'. The Cub Scouts must then try to touch the named article before they can be caught by the catchers. If caught they must become catchers too. The last one caught is the winner. The catchers must return to the centre of the room after each catching session.

(10) MAIN LINE STATION.

EQUIPMENT REQUIRED—One piece of chalk.

A track is drawn around the room in a series of loops and junctions. Take the illustration as but one example. All but

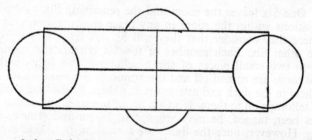

two of the Cub Scouts take up positions anywhere on the lines. These two Cub Scouts are appointed as catchers and the game is ready to begin. No one is allowed to run anywhere but on the lines, anyone seen treading on the floor instead of the lines is considered caught. All Cub Scouts caught leave the track and sit down by Akela. The two Cub Scout catchers should try to work as a team, trapping as many between them as possible.

(11) GASLAMPS.

EQUIPMENT REQUIRED—None.

This is a game of 'tig' with a difference. Use four catchers initially. When a Cub Scout is caught (i.e. touched) he stands still, legs astride as a 'gaslamp'. He remains in this position until released by some other free player, who releases him by crawling between his legs. When a person has been caught for the second time, he becomes a catcher too. The winner is the last player to be running free. The catchers should carry some distinguishing mark, i.e. those Cub Scouts wearing caps, so that they can be recognised.

(12) CATSTEP CATCHING.

EQUIPMENT REQUIRED—A piece of chalk.

A pattern of lines is drawn on the floor in a restricted area, i.e. about five metres (15 feet). This is important as the game can be exhausting. Here is an example of the type of pattern which can be used.

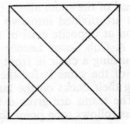

The Cub Scouts are told that they can travel only on the lines by catstepping, i.e. placing heel to toe alternately. See diagram. Two catchers are appointed who also must move along the lines by catstepping. The last boy caught is the winner.

(13) GUIDED MISSILES.

EQUIPMENT REQUIRED—Four blindfolds.

The Sixes occupy different corners of the room. One Cub Scout from each Six removes his shoes and is blindfolded. Each Six works out a method of giving instructions to their representative. They may use any words, whistles, etc., as long as they do not simply use the words right, left, straight on and about turn. At the command 'Go' the Sixes begin to call instructions to their Cub Scout, who must feel with his feet to locate a pea or similar article placed by Akela.

(14) UNDERSHOOT.

EQUIPMENT REQUIRED—One or two plastic footballs, chalk, a chair.

A track, two-thirds of a metre (two feet wide approx.), is drawn across the centre of the room. A further line is drawn at each end of the room about one metre from the wall. The Cub Scouts are divided into two teams and each team takes up position at opposite ends of the room within the chalked-off areas. A Cub Scout Leader walks up and down the centre area pushing a chair in front of him. This is a target and the object of the game is for the Cub Scouts to fire the ball by turning their backs on the target and firing at it between the legs. The teams are given a ball each and the scoring takes place as follows, one point for a hit on the chair, two points for a shot actually passing between the chair's legs, one point off for hitting the Cub Scout Leader.

(15) CLUTTER.

EQUIPMENT REQUIRED—About twenty beanbags or similar objects (see game 6), a piece of chalk.

Draw a chalk line about one metre (three feet) away from the wall and following the perimeter of the room. One Six are positioned in this area as the Sixer prescribes. The rest of the Cub Scouts take up position in the centre area and these are armed with the beanbags. The object of the game is for the Cub Scouts to throw the bags from the central area to the outer area. Here the defending Six must clear as much of the clutter as possible by throwing them back in the centre. A time limit is set and then the order to freeze is given. Penalties should be enforced on those who do not stop immediately, by counting three points against any who continue moving. Count up the beanbags in the defended area for the score against the defending team, and then change the Six. The Six having the least number of points against them are the winners.

(16) SKITTLE THEM OUT.

EQUIPMENT REQUIRED—Six skittles, two plastic footballs, chalk.

A four metre (twelve foot) circle is drawn in the centre of the room and one Six take up position inside the circle, each Cub Scout defending a skittle. Skittles can be improvised from plastic screw topped bottles containing a little water to make them steadier. Two plastic footballs are given to the remaining Cub Scouts and they have to attempt to skittle out the defending Six in as short a time as possible. Each defending Cub

Scout protects one skittle and when this is knocked down they must leave the circle, taking their skittle with them. Akela notes the time taken and then changes the defending Six. The Six surviving the longest are the winners. Defending Cub Scouts are not allowed to touch their skittles whilst defending, or to stand astride them. If they knock the skittle down themselves they are still counted out.

(17) FLYING HOOP.

EQUIPMENT REQUIRED—Four large hoops. N.B. these can be improvised by square lashing four poles together at the corners, or alternatively a large rope loop can be used.

Form four or two teams depending on the availability of hoops. The teams line up in Indian file and the Cub Scout at the front of the team holds the hoop. If a rope loop is used one Cub Scout is used from each team to help the front Cub Scout to hold the loop open. At the command 'Go', the first Cub Scout moves down the Six holding the hoop in such a way that the Cub Scouts can jump through it. When the back of the team is reached, the Cub Scout with the hoop runs to the front of the team and hands the hoop to number two. He in turn starts at the front of the line and the Six jump through it again and so on until everyone has run with the hoop. The hoop is then returned to the front of the team and they stand to attention to show that they have finished. The first Six to finish are declared the winners.

(18) MARBLE ROLLING.

EQUIPMENT REQUIRED—A bag of marbles, a piece of chalk.

The room is marked out as in the diagram.

Each team takes up its position behind the four lines

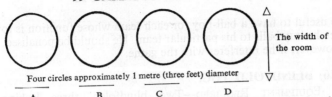

Four circles approximately 1 metre (three feet) diameter

The width of the room

A   B   C   D

'A', 'B', 'C', 'D', and the marbles are shared out. At the command 'Go' the first Cub Scout in each line rolls a marble at his team's target circle opposite. One Cub Scout from each team is positioned by the chalk circle and his purpose is to return to his team any marbles that do not come to rest within the circle. Akela sets a time limit and then the number of marbles at rest within the chalk circle are counted for each team, those with the highest number being declared the winners. If any marbles are dislodged by a poor or overhard throw, they must be returned to the team with other misses.

(19) ASTRIDE GOAL.

EQUIPMENT REQUIRED—2 plastic footballs.

The Cub Scouts are divided into two teams and these stand facing each other in two long lines holding hands. When the line is equally spaced the Cub Scouts drop hands and stand feet astride with their feet touching the feet of the Cub Scouts on either side of them. The teams should be approximately five to six metres apart (fifteen to twenty feet), and a plastic football is given to each team. When Akela says 'Go' the two teams try to score a goal by throwing the ball between the legs of the opposing team, or between two of the Cub Scouts. Two points are scored for a goal between the legs and one for a goal that passes between two of the opposing side. No points are scored if the ball passes a team over shoulder height. It is useful to have a ball-boy for each team whose function is to fetch stray balls to his particular team. He should be penalised, however, if he interferes with the game.

(20) BLINDFOLD TUG.

EQUIPMENT REQUIRED—Two blindfolds, three lashing ropes.

The Cub Scouts are divided into two teams and these stand back to back holding hands across the width of the room. Two Cub Scouts are chosen, one from each team, and these take up positions at opposite ends of the room and are blindfolded by a Cub Scout Leader. Three lengths of lashing rope are placed on the floor in various positions down the line of Cub Scouts so that one end of each lashing rope stretches into each half of the room. See diagram. The object of the game is for the two

blindfolded Cub Scouts to capture as many of the three lashing ropes as possible within two minutes. They score one point for each rope captured. The two lines of Cub Scouts are allowed to shout directions to their team member.

(21) MOUSETRAP.

Equipment Required—None.

One Six line the wall at one end of the room and are called 'mice'. The rest of the Cub Scouts line the opposite wall and maintaining contact with the wall stretch out their arms towards the mice. These are the mouse-traps. The mice are told to face the wall and whilst their backs are turned Akela chooses half of the mouse-traps approximately and these are considered 'set'. The mice then approach the traps and must choose to strike the outstretched fingers of the waiting Cub Scouts. If that particular trap is 'set', the Cub Scout concerned must attempt to catch the mouse. The mice are allowed to pretend to strike the outstretched fingers, as also the mouse-traps are allowed to pretend to give chase even if not 'set'. Each mouse that manages to reach the safety of his own wall scores a point for his Six, then the teams are changed round. The highest score denotes the winner.

(22) MARCHING MADNESS.

Equipment Required—Five pieces of rope or cloth long enough to tie two ankles together.

Each Six takes part in this competition in turn. They line up in Indian file and their ankles are tied together in the following manner. The leader's left leg is tied to number two's left leg. Number two's right leg is then tied to number three's right leg. Number three's left leg is then fastened to number four's left leg and so on. At the word 'Go' Akela sets a time limit of thirty seconds and the Six march as quickly as possible around the room. They must touch each corner of the room in turn and score a point for every corner they manage. Sixes are then changed and the Six with the most points are declared the winners.

B

(23) FIFTEEN SECOND DARKNESS.

EQUIPMENT REQUIRED—None.

One Six takes up position in the centre of the room and the remaining Cub Scouts line the four walls of the room. Akela turns off the lights and counts fifteen seconds. Then the lights are turned on again. The Cub Scouts in the centre of the room must attempt to reach the wall and be touching it when the lights go on. The others must attempt by catching and holding them to prevent this. When the lights go on, everyone must keep still whilst those touching the wall are counted. These gain one point each. Award points against anyone moving after the lights are put on. Those Cub Scouts touching the wall are not considered safe until the lights are put on, therefore the other Cub Scouts may remove them from the wall if they discover them in the dark.

(24) POT THE BALL.

EQUIPMENT REQUIRED—One plastic football.

Two teams are chosen and line opposite walls of the room. They stand feet apart, at least two-thirds of a metre between their feet (two feet). One person from each team is chosen as the 'kicker', and they go to the centre of the room. A coin is tossed to decide who begins. The winner places the ball on the centre spot and gently kicks it at the other team. The object is for him to cause the ball to either strike an opponent's foot or to cause the ball to pass between an opponent's legs. If successful, the person who has been knocked out may choose a position in his team's half of the room where he can sit down cross-legged. The object is for the defeated player to select a position that he judges will make the other side's 'kicker's' task more difficult. The position that he chooses is limited only by the fact that he must not be able to touch any other member of his team with his arms full outstretched. The 'kicker' may attempt to stop the ball on the rebound from his opponent's kick in a position he may consider to be advantageous. However, he may not move the ball, but must always shoot from wherever it comes to rest. The winners are the team who still have one or more Cub Scouts standing when all of the other team's Cub Scouts are eliminated.

(25) PEA PICKING.

EQUIPMENT REQUIRED—Four saucers, one plate or bowl, one packet of dried peas, one packet of straws, two boards, two dice, two shakers, one hat or cap.

In the centre of the room the bowl is placed and the dried peas are poured into it. On the floor next to it is placed the hat. The four saucers are then placed round the bowl and each Cub Scout is given a straw. The Cub Scouts sit in a large circle around the bowl. Two Cub Scout Leaders are equipped with a board, a shaker and a dice each. Each Six is allocated one saucer and the game is ready to start. The Cub Scout Leaders begin at opposite sides of the circle and walk round allowing each Cub Scout in turn to shake the dice. As soon as a six is thrown, the successful Cub Scout runs into the middle, puts on the hat and by sucking with his straw, begins to move as many peas as possible to his team's plate. He continues doing this until the hat is snatched from his head by a member of an opposing Six and so on. A time limit is set by Akela, and when this expires the saucer containing the most dry peas belongs to the winning Six.

(26) NOUGHTS AND CROSSES.

EQUIPMENT REQUIRED—Two dice, two shakers, a piece of white paper, a piece of cardboard, one felt-tipped pen, one chair.

The Cub Scouts are divided into two teams and the teams are named 'noughts and crosses'. Each team lines up in Indian file and they are numbered from front to back using the digits one to six. If there are more than six members in the team, the remainder are numbered from one to six similarly. Equidistant from the teams a chair is placed by a Cub Scout Leader. The card is propped up against the chair back so as to be easily visible by the teams. The white paper is fastened with sellotape and the matrix for noughts and crosses drawn on it with the felt-tipped pen. The dice and shakers are given to the leaders of the two teams and they are told which space each number can use on the noughts and crosses board. The spaces are allocated in the following way. Ones and twos are allowed to place their noughts or crosses depending which team they are in, on any of the four corner squares marked 'B' in the diagram. Numbers three, four and five may fill any of the four spaces between the corner squares marked 'C', and six is allowed to fill the centre square marked 'A' only.

B	C	B
C	A	C
B	C	B

The leaders of the teams are the first to throw the dice, and if they throw a number which corresponds with the number that they have been allocated, they are allowed to run up to the chair and choose one of their appointed squares, which is marked for them by a Cub Scout Leader. The result of the game is determined by the ordinary rules of noughts and crosses. Obviously if a certain number is required to enable a team to win, the team leader is justified in allowing the appropriate Cub Scout to throw the dice until he is successful.

(27) BREAKING THROUGH.

EQUIPMENT REQUIRED—About twelve blindfolds.

The Cub Scouts are divided into two teams and one team is blindfolded. This team stands feet astride across the width of the room, with their feet apart and touching the Cub Scout's feet on either side of them. Thus they form a continuous cordon. The cordon try to touch the others in passing. When all the Cub Scouts are either captured or safely through the cordon, the number of captures are counted and then the roles are reversed. The winning team effect the most captures.

(28) CROSSFIRE.

EQUIPMENT REQUIRED—Three skittles, three plastic footballs, a watch with second hand and a piece of chalk.

Three one metre (three feet) circles are spaced out along an imaginary line cutting across the centre of the room. A line is drawn parallel to the three circles at each end of the room three metres (nine feet) away from the wall. See diagram.

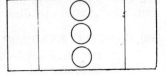

A skittle is placed in each of the three circles and one Cub Scout is chosen to defend them. The rest of the Cub Scouts are divided into two teams and take up position in the two areas within the chalk marks at the ends of the room. These are armed with the three footballs and Akela takes note of the time. At the word 'Go' the Cub Scouts at the two ends of the room attempt to knock down the three skittles. The Cub Scout's turn ends the moment that at any time all three skittles are down, Akela noting the time taken. The defending Cub Scout is allowed to replace any skittle knocked down and may defend the skittles still standing, but may not stand astride the skittle.

(29) ATISHOO !

EQUIPMENT REQUIRED—Three blindfolds.

All but one Six join hands and form a large circle. Inside this circle go the remaining Six, plus one representative each from the three or more Sixes forming the circle. These three representatives are blindfolded. The object of the game is for these three blindfolded Cub Scouts to catch as many of the Six in the circle for their own Six as possible. As Cub Scouts are captured they are removed by a Cub Scout Leader. From time to time Akela says 'Atishoo' and all the Cub Scouts still free within the circle must answer 'Atishoo', this of course is designed to help the blindfolded Cub Scouts to locate the free Cub Scouts. Sixes and Six representatives are changed round and captures totalled to determine the winning Six.

(30) DANCING BEARS.

EQUIPMENT REQUIRED—None.

The Cub Scouts pair off and face each other. They each

grasp the other's forearms and one of each pair lightly stands on the other one's toes. After a quick practice at walking like this the pairs attempt to nudge and bump other pairs, causing them to overbalance. The last pair of balanced Cub Scouts are the winners. Any team putting a foot down or overbalancing is removed from the game area by a Cub Scout Leader.

(31) PEA WALK.

EQUIPMENT REQUIRED—One packet of dried peas.

A game for dark nights. Akela scatters a number of dried peas over the floor and the lights are turned off. The Sixes must collect as many of the peas as possible using the sense of touch before the light is turned on again. The Sixer counts his Six's peas and a Cub Scout Leader rechecks the highest score, to determine the winner.

(32) CAT'S CRADLE.

EQUIPMENT REQUIRED—A watch.

This is a variation of cat and mouse. One Six are designated as the mice and a cat is chosen. The rest of the Cub Scouts form as large a circle as possible holding hands. The object of the game is for the cat to catch all the mice as quickly as possible. The circle of Cub Scouts assists the cat in this by allowing the cat to pass easily between them, whilst attempting to hinder the mice. Akela notes how long it takes to catch all the mice and then the Six is changed and so on. The longest time taken denotes the winning Six.

(33) SMUGGLER'S GOLD.

EQUIPMENT REQUIRED—Watch with second hand, small pieces of paper, a pen.

The Cub Scouts are divided into two teams. One team leaves the room with a Cub Scout Leader and these are given small pieces of paper with one letter of the alphabet written on it. Akela draws two lines across the room two metres (six feet) apart and in such a way that the two lines form a barrier between the door and the wall opposite the door. The second team take up position within this area. The object of the game is for the team outside the room to conceal somewhere about their person (within reason!) the piece of paper and then entering through the door they attempt to break through the cordon of Cub Scouts to reach Akela who is in the area behind the cordon. Akela collects the piece of paper, and the Cub Scout may safely return to the Cub Scout Leader, who gives him another one and so on. It will help the paper-carrying team if Akela will sort the letters as they arrive in such a way as to be able to tell the successful Cub Scout what additional letters are still required to complete the alphabet. The defending team must attempt to catch the others whilst on the wall and hold them there until they have counted three. If successful in this they are allowed to search the captured Cub Scouts to see if they can locate the hidden paper. Points are awarded for every letter successfully smuggled or captured within a time limit set by Akela. Give five bonus points if the attacking team succeed in completing the alphabet.

(34) SKIP TO MY LOU.

EQUIPMENT REQUIRED—Four skipping ropes.

The Sixes line up at one end of the room behind their Sixers, in Indian file. Each Sixer is given a skipping rope. At the command 'Go' from Akela, the Sixers run and touch the far wall of the room and then have to skip ten before running

back to their Six and handing over to number two and so on.
The first team to complete these actions and stand to attention
are the winners.

(35) CIRCLE TUG OF WAR.

EQUIPMENT REQUIRED—One lashing rope.

Each Cub Scout pairs off with another member of his own
Six and then the pairs form a circle with each Six having a
quarter of it. The circle is divided into quarters by chalk lines.
See the diagram.

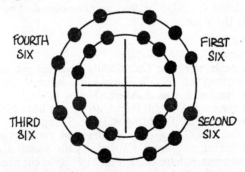

The two ends of the lashing rope are tied together and the
loop thus formed is placed in the centre of the circle. The Cub
Scouts nearest the centre are named number ones and those on
the outside number twos. Akela says 'Go' and number twos
race clockwise round the circle until they arrive back at their
partner. Here they go through his legs and attempt to snatch
the lashing rope into their own quarter of the circle. If a tug
of war ensues, the other members of the Sixes concerned may

help their team member by pulling him around the waist. The number twos then become number ones and so on. Akela keeps the score.

(36) SAFE ISLAND.
EQUIPMENT REQUIRED—None.

One Cub Scout is chosen to be 'He' and chases the others. Anyone touched is caught and becomes a safe island. To do this he kneels down on the floor. Any Cub Scout touching him cannot be caught. However, from time to time Akela calls out 'Change' and anyone touching a safe island must leave that island and either dodge or find another island. The last one running is the winner.

(37) FUNFAIR.
EQUIPMENT REQUIRED—None.

Akela explains to the Cub Scouts what actions they must perform when given certain commands. Roundabouts: They must run clockwise round Akela. Helter Skelter: They spin round on the spot. Weightlifter: Cub Scouts hold both hands above their heads as if holding weights. Swing-boats: They lie on their fronts holding their ankles and rock. High-diver: They fall flat on the floor. Fat-lady: Cub Scouts stand legs astride and arms outstretched. Point out different areas of the room where the Cub Scouts must run if the commands Dodgems, Big Wheel or Side-shows are given. The last Cub Scout to obey any command drops out. The last one in being the winner.

(38) TRANSPORT COMMAND.
EQUIPMENT REQUIRED—None.

Teach the Cub Scouts how to make a three-handed seat. See diagram.

Cub Scout 2

Free hand supports
the back of seated
Cub Scout.

Cub Scout 1

Divide the Cub Scouts into two teams. In each team half of
the Cub Scouts are 'carriers' and the rest have to be carried.
The carriers pair off and construct three-handed seats. At the
command 'Go' from Akela the first of the three-handed seats
from each team ferry one other member of their team to the
far wall and back again. Then the second three-hand seat
ferries a further team member and so on. The first team to have
successfully ferried the whole of their team the length of the
room and back are declared the winners.

(39) CATCH HIM BY THE TAIL.

EQUIPMENT REQUIRED—Two blindfolds, one watch, one
lashing rope at least three metres (nine feet) long.

All but three of the Cub Scouts form a large circle holding
hands and having their feet apart. Two of the remaining three
are blindfolded, the other has a long length of rope tied to his
belt. The object of this game is for this boy to avoid being

caught by either of the other two blindfolded ones. All three Cub Scouts must maintain physical contact with the circle of Cub Scouts at all times. However, they can move round inside or outside the circle. The starting time is noted and the game begins. The Cub Scout with the tail is not allowed to touch his tail at all, and if it becomes caught, he must retrace his steps to free it. The blindfold Cub Scouts, however, may if they find the rope, hold it and follow it to its owner. The length of time taken is the record and is challenged by other catchers. No Cub Scout in the circle is allowed to deliberately trap the rope.

(40) DRIVE IT HOME.

EQUIPMENT REQUIRED—Two old shoes or objects of a similar weight. About twenty missiles, for example beanbags or rolled and sellotaped balls of paper.

The Cub Scouts are divided into two teams and each team lines one half of the same wall. In the centre of the room opposite each team are placed the two shoes. The Cub Scouts are then armed with the beanbags. The object of the game is for each team of Cub Scouts to bombard their shoe and cause it to be knocked against the opposite wall before the other team can do likewise. Missiles may only be thrown by Cub Scouts maintaining contact with the wall. Beanbags may be retrieved by any member of the team as long as he does not interfere with the other team's throws.

(41) STEPPING STONES.

EQUIPMENT REQUIRED—Eight tin cans, preferably with lids, i.e. dried milk containers or coffee tins, a piece of chalk.

Four two metre (six feet) circles are drawn on the floor two metres (six feet) apart in the form of a square, i.e. one circle on each of the imaginary square's four corners. One Six occupies each circle and is equipped with two of the cans. Akela sets a time limit and the Cub Scouts must attempt to cross from one circle to the next in a clockwise direction, using the cans as stepping stones. The skill in the game is to balance on one tin whilst moving the second tin forward and so on. All the Cub Scouts who overbalance and touch the floor are considered to have been eaten by the sharks and must retire from the game. When a Cub Scout successfully crosses to an island, he must return the two tins by rolling them on the floor back to his Six. If one of the tins is lost in this way by a bad roll, one of the Cub Scouts must sacrifice his life by retrieving it and so on. Points are awarded in the following way. Ten points for the Six who have progressed the farthest, six points for the second team, four for the third and two for the fourth. Deduct one point for each dead Cub Scout.

(42) CATCHERS.

EQUIPMENT REQUIRED—One plastic bottle.

The Sixes form a small circle, one Six to each quarter. In the centre Akela spins a bottle. When this comes to rest it will point to one of the Sixes. These Cub Scouts are then the 'catchers' and must catch as many of the other Cub Scouts as possible before they can reach the safety of a wall. Put the wall immediately behind each Six out of bounds to that Six, thus forcing them to run further to safety and insist that no one is allowed to run before the bottle has come to rest. Keep a score of successful catches.

(43) THE STRAIGHT AND NARROW.

EQUIPMENT REQUIRED—Two pillows or sacks full of soft rags or paper. Chalk.

A straight line is drawn down the centre of the room in chalk. The Cub Scouts are divided into two teams, each team taking up position at opposite ends of the room. The front member of each team is armed with a cushion or similar item and the game is ready to begin. The first member of each team walks down the chalk trail, being careful to maintain contact with the chalk line all the time. On meeting they attempt to knock their opponent off the line. One foot off is sufficient to eliminate a competitor. The victor stays on the line until he loses a battle. The last team to have someone left on the line is the winner.

(44) FOUR GOAL CRAB FOOTBALL.

EQUIPMENT REQUIRED—One plastic football.

The Sixes are allocated one wall each which they must defend as a goal. The Cub Scouts take up position anywhere on the floor in the crab position. See diagram.

The object of the game is for the teams to attempt to score as many goals as possible on their opponent's walls whilst at the same time attempting to defend their own. To score a goal the ball must strike the wall below the height of one metre (three feet). If the walls are uneven in length change around the allocation of goal to ensure fairness.

(45) SPEED TRIAL.

EQUIPMENT REQUIRED—A watch with a second hand.

The Pack form a large circle. Two Cub Scouts are chosen and these take up position outside the circle and on exactly opposite sides. At the word 'Go' from Akela they race round the circle in a clockwise direction for exactly one minute. When the time has elapsed, the Cub Scout who is judged to have been catching the other one is declared the winner. Then the Cub Scouts are changed.

(46) INVENTING.

EQUIPMENT REQUIRED—A watch with a second hand, two chairs.

The Sixes line up in Indian file as for a relay and a chair is placed opposite each team at the other end of the room, away from the wall. A Cub Scout Leader takes up position sitting on each chair. Akela sets a time limit, for example three minutes and says 'Go'. In this time the Cub Scouts must move one at a time up to and around their own chair and back to their team. The object of this game is for the Cub Scouts to invent as many varied methods of covering this distance as possible in the allotted time. For example, walking, hopping, running, walking backwards, holding ankles, moving as a crab, etc. No method must be duplicated by any one team and the order of the team must be adhered to. If time is lost in thinking it cannot be avoided. After the time expires the total number of ways achieved are totalled by the Cub Scout Leaders and the winners are the Six who devised the highest number of ways.

(47) VALLEY OF DEATH.

EQUIPMENT REQUIRED—Two long ropes about six metre (nineteen feet), six paper clubs, six blindfolds.

A roped-off area is made by four Cub Scout Leaders, these stretch the two six metre ropes down the centre of the room about four metre (twelve feet) apart, as in the diagram.

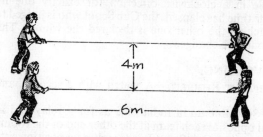

The area between the ropes is termed the 'Valley of Death'. One Six is blindfolded, armed with paper clubs and positioned in the valley. The other teams must attempt to pass one at a time through the valley without being struck with a paper club. If they are struck they count as a point to the blindfolded Six. Change Sixes and total up the scores to determine the winners. The ropes prevent the blindfolded Six from straying outside the valley.

(48) KNOTTY PROBLEMS.

EQUIPMENT REQUIRED—One short length of string per Cub Scout. Chalk.

Each Six take their allocation of string into their corner and when Akela says 'Go' they attempt to shorten the lengths of the string as much as possible in one minute by tying knots. Akela then calls 'Stop', after which the lengths of knotted string are taken by one Cub Scout to the nearest Six in a clockwise direction. Then Akela once again says 'Go' and the Cub Scouts have three minutes to remove as many of the knots as possible. When the three minutes have elapsed, each Sixer takes his lengths of string to Akela, who stretches them out one at a time on the floor starting at the wall and making a chalk mark at the end of each length. The total length from the wall is denoted by the last chalk mark and the other Sixes' string is compared to denote the winner.

(49) CHARIOT DRIVING.

EQUIPMENT REQUIRED—Chalk, two lengths of rope or string about two metre (six feet) long, six blindfolds.

A figure-of-eight track is drawn upon the floor one metre (three feet) wide, as in the diagram.

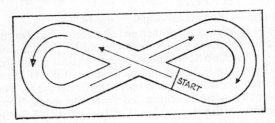

All but one member of the Six is blindfolded and stand in Indian file behind the start of the track. The Cub Scout who is not blindfolded takes up position at the back of the line. He holds one end each of the two ropes/string, the other ends of which are fastened around the elbows of the leading Cub Scout. The driver takes his cue from Akela and steers the blindfolded chariot once around the track, pulling on the two ropes to indicate changes of direction. A point is deducted for every time the chariot crosses the track boundary. The time taken is recorded by Akela. Points are awarded for the fastest circuit as follows, first—four points, second—three and so on. The highest score at the end is the winner.

(50) WHISTLE AND OUT.

EQUIPMENT REQUIRED—One whistle, one plastic ball.

The Cub Scouts form a circle and begin passing the plastic ball from one to another across the circle. If anyone drops a catch he must fall out of the game, unless the throw was a bad one. A Cub Scout Leader turns his back on the game and from time to time blows a whistle. Anyone holding the ball when the whistle is blown also falls out. The last one in is the winner.

(51) LAST TO SCORE.

EQUIPMENT REQUIRED—One plastic ball.

A goal is formed three metres (nine feet) wide against one of the longest walls of the room and a goal-keeper is appointed. The rest of the Cub Scouts play football against each other, all attempting to score. When anyone is successful and scores he becomes temporarily safe and retires from the game. The last Cub Scout to score is eliminated from the game. Then the game restarts with everyone but this eliminated Cub Scout in it and so on. As this is a slow game to reach a conclusion, it can be speeded up by eliminating the last four or six Cub Scouts each time, The last pair play off to determine the winner.

(52) BOTTLE CHANGE.

EQUIPMENT REQUIRED—One plastic bottle.

The Cub Scouts sit in a large circle on the floor with the exception of one Cub Scout who takes up position outside the circle. The bottle is placed in the centre of the circle and given a spin. When it settles and points with the neck and the bottom at two seated Cub Scouts, these must change places with each other. The Cub Scout outside the circle must attempt to occupy one of these two places. If a Cub Scout is displaced in this way, he takes up position outside the circle and so on. Whilst the bottle is in motion, the Cub Scout outside the circle is not allowed to move.

(53) CIRCLE FOUR GOALS.

EQUIPMENT REQUIRED—One ball.

One Cub Scout is selected from each Six and then the Sixes form a circle holding hands, each Six forming a quarter of the circle. Each Six is allotted the wall behind their quarter of the circle as a goal and they must defend it. The object of the game is for the Cub Scouts in the circle to attempt to score a goal by kicking the ball out of the circle and against any of their opponents' goals. The Cub Scouts outside the circle must attempt to prevent a goal being scored on their wall by stopping the ball and dropping it back inside the circle at the feet of their team. They may also attempt to prevent the other three Cub Scouts from saving a goal by obstructing them, holding them and so on.

(54) FLICK.

EQUIPMENT REQUIRED—Four spent matchsticks.

The Sixes line up in Indian file for a relay. A chalk line is drawn in front of each team. The Sixer of each team is given a matchstick and the game is ready to begin. They flick the matchstick in the direction of the far wall, run to where it has fallen and repeat the action until the wall is reached. Then the leader runs back to his Six and passes the match to number two and so on. The first team to finish are the winners.

(55) WHAT IS IT?

EQUIPMENT REQUIRED—None.

Akela or a Cub Scout Leader stands in front of the Cub Scouts and mimes some object he wants brought to him. The first Six to produce the correct object scores a point and so on.

(56) MASS HAND TENNIS.

EQUIPMENT REQUIRED—One ball, preferably plastic medium size, a piece of chalk.

The Cub Scouts are divided into two teams and the room is divided by means of a chalk line, lengthwise, one team taking up position in each half. A coin is tossed to determine which team starts and they are given the ball. The object of the game is for the team with the ball to 'serve' it by throwing it up in the air and striking it with the flat of the hand into their opponents' half. It must not be hit too hard, causing it to strike the roof or the wall, but rather it must bounce in their opponents' area. The other team return the ball by striking it with the flat of their hands in turn. If the ball does strike the wall without bouncing, or hits the roof, it counts as a point to the other team. If the ball is not hit sufficiently hard to carry it over the line before it bounces, or if the ball is simply missed, again it is a point to the other team. Score the points as in real tennis, i.e. love, fifteen, thirty, forty, game.

(57) TEAM BOWLING.

EQUIPMENT REQUIRED—Nine or better still eighteen skittles (plastic screw-top bottles quarter full of water are ideal). One or two balls, depending on the number of skittles. Two pieces of paper, two pencils.

The Cub Scouts are divided into two teams. The two teams take up poisition at the same end of the room, each equipped with a ball ready to bowl. Opposite each team at the other end of the room a Cub Scout Leader sets up nine skittles. If there are only nine skittles available, the teams will take it in turn to bowl. However, the game is more exciting if there are two sets of skittles as a race element can be introduced. The following design in numbers is written on each of the two

```
              9
          8       8
       7     7     7
     6    6    6    6
   5    5    5    5    5
     4    4    4    4
       3    3    3
         2    2
            1
```

pieces of paper and a Sixer is given the paper and pencil to do the recording for his team.

The object of the game is for the Sixer to cross off from his list the number of skittles knocked down by his team with each bowl. For example, if six skittles are knocked down one of the sixes on the list is crossed out. Akela sets a time limit after which the remaining numbers on each list are totalled up, the team having the lowest total being the winners. The two Cub Scout Leaders replace the skittles after each bowl.

(58) COFFIN BOWLING.

Equipment Required—As in Game Fifty-seven.

The game is set up exactly as in Game Fifty-seven, with one exception, and that is that only one set of skittles is required. A coin is tossed to determine which team bowls first. The first representative from this team then bowls and as long as some of the skittles are knocked down nothing further occurs on that player's turn. The skittles knocked down are left down and the first player from the second team takes his turn and so on until all the skittles are down, when they are all replaced again. If, however, a player misses entirely with his shot then one line of his team's coffin is drawn as in the diagram.

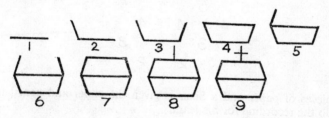

The first team to have its coffin fully drawn is considered to have lost the game. If a member of one of the teams manages to knock down all the remaining pins on his turn a line is added to the other team's coffin.

(59) INDOOR BEACHBALL.

EQUIPMENT REQUIRED—One plastic football, a piece of chalk.

The Cub Scouts are divided into two teams and line opposite walls of the room, sitting down facing each other. They are then numbered from left to right. In the centre of the room two lines are drawn across the width of the room and parallel to the two teams, one metre (three feet) apart. A ball is then placed centrally between the two lines. Akela calls a number and the two Cub Scouts concerned run out and push the ball over their opponent's line. If one Cub Scout arrives ahead of the other, he may push the ball over the line just as if the other boy was there. No other part of the body may be used to push the ball except the hands and these may not be used as a fist.

(60) HOP AROUND.

EQUIPMENT REQUIRED—One piece of chalk.

A square large enough to hold all the Cub Scouts at once is drawn in each corner of the room. Each of the four squares is given a letter 'A', 'B', 'C', 'D', which is written in them. The Cub Scouts all enter square 'A'. Akela then calls out a letter of the alphabet and if the letter called refers to one of the other squares the Cub Scouts must hop to that square. Cub Scouts are eliminated from the game by being the last one to arrive at the new square, putting both feet on the floor whilst crossing the room to a new square, overbalancing, or setting off for a new square when Akela has called some other letter of the alphabet than the ones written in the squares. The last one in is the winner.

(61) BALLOON POLO.

EQUIPMENT REQUIRED—Two balloons, two old towels or equivalent, i.e. old sheets, etc.

The Cub Scouts are divided into two teams and each team member pairs off with a partner. It is better if a small Cub Scout pairs off with a large one. Then each team in their pairs line opposite side walls of the room and are numbered left to right, one number for each pair. A goal is constructed at each end of the room about four metres (twelve feet) wide, using chairs, etc. In the centre of the room is placed a softly blown up balloon and just in front of each team is placed an old towel or equivalent. Akela calls a number and the smaller of the two Cub Scouts in each pair arms himself with the towel and mounts pick-a-back upon his partner. The object of the game is for the mounted Cub Scout to sweep the balloon by means of the towel into the opponent's goal, thus scoring a point for his team. No feet are allowed to kick the balloon.

(62) TIME TO WHOAH !

EQUIPMENT REQUIRED—Four blindfolds, a piece of chalk.

Each Six takes up position in a different corner of the room. The largest Cub Scout from each Six is chosen and sent to Akela in the centre of the room, where they are blindfolded to act as their Six's horse. Each Six decides in what order their members will play the game and line up. Akela then marks on the floor equidistant from the four horses a different symbol for each Six; for example the initial letter of each Six's colour could be used. Akela calls 'Go' and the first person in each team runs out, mounts his horse and guides it by turning the Cub Scout's head in the direction he wants him to go. When the pair reaches their symbol the rider calls 'Whoah!' The first pair to successfully arrive win a point for their team. It is advisable to have a Cub Scout Leader positioned to prevent crashes.

(63) HEADHUNTERS.

EQUIPMENT REQUIRED—Six large cardboard boxes or alternatively plastic bowls. About twenty beanbags or sello-taped paper balls, A piece of chalk.

Divide the room in half by drawing a chalk line across the centre. Position one Six in one half and the remaining Sixes in the second half of the room. The first Six are equipped with cardboard boxes, taking one each and supporting them on their heads. Three or four Cub Scouts are selected from the remaining Sixes and these go into the same half of the room as the Cub Scouts with the boxes. The Sixes are armed with the beanbags and must attempt to throw or lob them into one of the boxes of the other Six. This Six must do their utmost to prevent them from doing this by keeping constantly moving, presenting a difficult target. The three or four Cub Scouts in their half of the room must return the beanbags that have missed the target to the throwers. Akela decides on a time limit and when this has expired the number of heads collected are counted to determine that Sixes score, i.e., the number of beanbags successfully lobbed into the boxes. Roles are then changed and the Six having collected the least number of beanbags is declared the winner.

(64) MARBLE HE.

Equipment Required—A bag of marbles.

One Cub Scout is chosen and given a marble. He is positioned in the centre of the room and the rest of the Pack run anywhere in the remaining area. Akela calls 'Freeze' and all the Cub Scouts stand perfectly still. The Cub Scout with the marble places the marble on the floor and strikes it with the side of the forefinger (see diagram) towards the feet of any Cub Scout he thinks he can hit. If successful this Cub Scout joins him in the centre of the room and is given a marble. The first Cub Scout retrieves his marble and the free Cub Scouts may run around and change position until Akela orders 'Freeze' again and so on. The last Cub Scout free is the winner.

(65) TEN UP.

Equipment Required—Four blindfolds, one bag of dried peas.

The Cub Scouts form a large circle holding hands. One Cub Scout from each Six enters the circle and is blindfolded. Forty-five dried peas are scattered in the circle and the game begins. The blindfolded Cub Scouts must race each other to be the first to collect ten peas, when they must shout 'Ten Up', the first one to do so scoring one for his team. It is important that the number of peas on the floor should be only a few more than is required to give them ten each. Any peas knocked outside the circle should be replaced by a Cub Scout Leader.

(66) CHAIR LEG RELAY.

EQUIPMENT REQUIRED—Two chairs, two containers, one bag of peas, a watch.

The Cub Scouts are divided into two teams and line up in Indian file at one end of the room. A container of some kind is placed beside each team and opposite them at the other end of the room is placed a chair upon which is sat a Cub Scout Leader. In the centre of the room Akela stands with a bag of dried peas. See diagram.

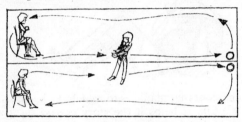

At the word 'Go' the first member of each team runs to the chair and creeps through between the chair's legs. Then he runs to Akela, who gives him a dried pea, he runs back to his team, placing the pea in the container and thus setting off the next runner and so on. Akela sets a time limit and when this expires the team having the most peas within their container are the winners.

(67) SNATCH.

EQUIPMENT REQUIRED—A number of objects that can be thrown without breaking, for example beanbags or paper balls.

Akela sits on a chair in the centre of the room armed with a

number of beanbags. The Cub Scouts sit on the floor close to
Akela's legs. Akela then tells a story punctuating it frequently
with the word 'Snatch'. Each time the word 'Snatch' is said
Akela throws one of the beanbags out into the room, the Cub
Scouts moving as crabs to recover it. See diagram.

The Cub Scout that manages to snatch the beanbag scores a
point for his Six. It helps if the story carries on despite the
skirmishing of the Cub Scouts, two or three articles being
raced for at one time. The Cub Scouts must return the beanbag
to Akela to score the point.

(68) HEAVE HO !

EQUIPMENT REQUIRED—A piece of chalk.

The Cub Scouts are divided into two teams. A line is drawn
across the centre of the room and each team takes up possession
of one of the two halves thus formed. The object of the game
is for members of each team to attempt to pull members of the
other team over the line into their half of the room, thus
eliminating them from the game. To avoid Cub Scouts hanging
back in the safety of their areas Akela from time to time

says 'Touch'. At this command everyone on both sides must touch the centre line within five seconds and of course may catch others doing this. The judging is performed by Cub Scout Leaders and must be very strict. If a Cub Scout in his eagerness to catch a member of the other team puts a foot over the line, he is caught himself and eliminated. However, it is quite all right for arms, etc., to cross the line.

(69) JAPANESE WRESTLING.

EQUIPMENT REQUIRED—A piece of chalk.

A chalk circle about two metres (six feet) across is drawn on the floor and a knockout competition is run on the following lines. Two competitors enter the circle and face each other standing feet astride. They reach around each other and grasp with both hands the belt and trouser top of their opponent, resting their heads on each other's shoulders. At the command 'Go' they attempt to push or pull their opponent out of the circle, thus winning a point for their Six. Give an extra point to the champion of champions. No tripping is allowed.

(70) FOOT HUNTING.

EQUIPMENT REQUIRED—None.

The Sixes take up position at separate corners of the room and face each other kneeling down. They remove their shoes and the game is ready to begin. The Sixes converge on each other, walking on their knees. The object of the game is for each Cub Scout to attempt to grasp the foot or ankle of an opponent. If they achieve this they call out 'Foot', attracting the attention of a Cub Scout Leader. The Cub Scout caught by the foot is eliminated from the game and so on. The last Cub Scout in is the winner for his Six. No standing up is allowed.

(71) HORSEY CORNERS.

EQUIPMENT REQUIRED—None.

The Sixes line up in Indian file in the centre of the room each Six facing their Six corner. Each Six pairs off in size, a large Cub Scout with a small one as far as possible. At the command 'Go' by Akela, the small boy jumps up on the back of the large one, who acts as the horse. The four pairs of horse and rider head for their Six corner. On arriving there, the rider touches the corner and then they set off in a clockwise direction around the room touching the remaining three corners. Then they return to the centre of the room setting off the next pair and so on. The first Six to finish are the winners.

(72) GUARD THE CHAIR.

EQUIPMENT REQUIRED—A chair, a plastic football.

A chair is placed in the centre of the room and a Cub Scout chosen to guard it. The other Cub Scouts form a large circle around the chair. The object of the game is for these Cub Scouts to hit the chair by throwing the ball whilst the defending Cub Scout tries to prevent this for as long as possible. The time is taken by Akela and constitutes a record that the other Cub Scouts must attempt to beat. The Cub Scout who is successful in hitting the chair may be chosen as the one who replaces the defender.

(73) FEATHER DROP.

EQUIPMENT REQUIRED—A feather or piece of fluffed-out cotton wool.

Akela stands in the centre of the room armed with a feather or fluffed-out piece of cotton wool. The Cub Scouts form a large circle around him and the game is ready to begin. He calls a Cub Scout by name and drops the feather. The Cub Scout must attempt to catch the feather before it reaches the floor. If successful he may drop the feather and call the next name, if unsuccessful he returns to his place in the circle.

(74) BACKWARD CROW SHOT.

EQUIPMENT REQUIRED—One plastic football.

Each Six select a wall and stand along it spaced out. They face the wall and stand legs astride about an arm's length away from it. A coin is tossed by Akela to determine which Six begins and the plastic football is given to them. The Cub Scout with the ball must shoot at any member of another Six by bending down and throwing the ball between his legs. If the ball then hits the foot of an opponent, or passes between his feet, he is out and must sit down. No attempt to protect his legs is allowed. If a Cub Scout moves his feet to avoid a throw he is out also. The last Cub Scout standing is the winner for his Six.

(75) LOOTING.

EQUIPMENT REQUIRED—A piece of chalk, a packet of dried peas and a watch, four small containers.

Four two metre (six feet) circles are drawn on the floor about two metres (six feet) away from the walls in each Six corner. In the centre of each circle are piled one hundred dried peas. One Cub Scout from each Six guards his Six's peas. Each Six has a container which is kept by a Cub Scout Leader. Akela gives the signal to start and the Sixes must attempt to 'loot' the peas from some other Six circle. They do this by dashing into the circle and out again without being touched by the defender. If they are touched by the defender they must drop out of the game. Cub Scout Leaders must judge whether or not a Cub Scout has been caught and if insufficient Cub Scout Leaders are available to watch all four circles, it is better to reduce the number of teams and circles. If any peas are captured they are placed in the Six container. Akela sets a time limit of around four minutes and then the captured peas are counted up to determine the winners.

(76) COMPASS ROOM.

EQUIPMENT REQUIRED—A piece of chalk.

The room is marked out with the four cardinal points of the compass, one to each wall. All the Cub Scouts stand in the centre of the room and the game is ready to begin. Akela gives the command 'Spin' and the Cub Scouts close their eyes and spin round. Akela then cries 'North' or 'East', etc., and the Cub Scouts stop spinning, open their eyes and attempt to go to the point chosen. The last Cub Scout arriving there drops out. This is repeated until one Cub Scout is left, who is the winner. Then try the game with eight compass points, using the corners of the room for NE, SW, etc.

(77) TARGET HOOP.

EQUIPMENT REQUIRED—A hoop, or construct a square by square-lashing four sticks together. Two balls, a piece of chalk, two ropes, each of which should be long enough to stretch half way across the room.

A centre line is drawn across the room from side to side and parallel to this on either side of it four metres (twelve feet) away two further lines are drawn across the room. A hoop is laid on the centre line and two ropes are attached to it, one on either side. A Cub Scout Leader stands at each end of the centre line, each holding one end of the two ropes. By pulling in on the rope and letting it out, the hoop can be drawn to and fro across the room. The Cub Scouts are divided into two teams and they take up position behind one of the two lines four metres away from the centre line, facing the opposing team. A ball is given to each team and the game is ready to begin. The object of the game is for the teams to score a goal by bouncing the ball within the hoop. The Cub Scout Leaders manipulating the hoop try to prevent this by pulling the hoop at different speeds, reversing the direction of pulling, etc. Akela keeps the score and the team scoring the most goals are the winners.

(78) TRAIN MIX.

EQUIPMENT REQUIRED—None.

Each Six lines up behind its Sixer in a corner of the room. They each hold the waist of the Cub Scout in front of them. Akela notes some object in the room; for example the flag, writes it down backwards and then reads the word backwards, in this case 'galf'. The first Six to work out what the object is must move as a train to it and touch it to gain a point.

(79) ALLEY PASS BALL.

EQUIPMENT REQUIRED—A piece of chalk, two small balls.

Parallel lines are drawn across the centre of the room two metres (six feet) apart. Two further lines are drawn, one on either side and parallel to the first two lines three metres (nine feet) away from them. The Cub Scouts are divided into two teams and line up facing each other behind the two outer lines. One ball is given to each team and the object of the game is for the Cub Scouts in possession of the ball to bounce it

within the area marked out by the middle two lines, causing
the ball to pass between the defence of the other team. They
field the ball and return it in a similar manner. The scoring
is as follows:

If the thrower misses the parallel line area, 1 point to the
other team.

If the defending team fail to catch it, 1 point to the attackers.

If the ball hits the walls in the defending team's area they
may still catch it. It is still in play until it actually hits the
floor.

(80) FOUR CORNER VOLLEY BALL.

EQUIPMENT REQUIRED—A plastic football, a piece of chalk.

A centre-line is drawn both across and down the room, thus
dividing it into four quarters. A Six takes up occupation of each
corner and Akela tosses a coin to decide who is to serve. The
winning Six serve the ball by hitting it with the flat of the
hand into any of the other three quarters of the room. The ball
must travel at above shoulder height or a point is awarded
to the receiving Six. They also receive a point if the ball is too
high and strikes the roof, or too fast and hits a boundary wall.
If, however, the ball is correctly served it must be hit out of
the new Six's corner again with the flat of the hand and above
shoulder height. The receiving Six may hit the ball up to four
times within their own area before losing a point to the last
Six to have had the ball. If the ball strikes the floor it is a point
to the last Six to have had possession. Serve in rotation.

(81) NOUGHTS AND VERY CROSSES.

EQUIPMENT REQUIRED—A piece of chalk.

A noughts and crosses design is drawn in the centre of the

room. The nine spaces should be just large enough to accommodate one Cub Scout. The Cub Scouts are divided into two teams, one at each end of the room and they are numbered from left to right. One team is named crosses and the other is called noughts. Akela calls a number and the Cub Scouts concerned run into the centre of the room. They may select separate spaces to stand and a Cub Scout Leader marks the two squares chosen with the appropriate sign, or they may contest a square, attempting to push each other off the space. If a contest develops Akela should turn his back on it for a predetermined number of seconds then say 'Freeze', the Cub Scout in possession or having more possession than the other wins the space. As before the other Cub Scout must reselect a space from those remaining. The object is, of course, to score a point by gaining a straight line of three noughts or crosses.

(82) BLIND TUG OF WAR.

EQUIPMENT REQUIRED—A blindfold, a piece of chalk, a short thick piece of rope.

The Cub Scouts are divided into two teams and these line opposite ends of the room. A line is then drawn across the centre of the room dividing the two teams. Beginning at the left hand side of each team, a Cub Scout Leader chalks a number at the feet of each Cub Scout in turn, beginning at one and working up. Akela selects a Cub Scout from one of the teams and blindfolds him, placing in his hands one end of the rope. All the Cub Scouts in the opposing team then change places, standing on the numbers chalked on the floor. The blindfold Cub Scout selects a number, the Cub Scout thus chosen becomes his opponent and prepares to pull at the other end of the rope. A tug of war is held and only after the result is determined should the blindfolded Cub Scout see who his opponent was! If you have an obvious champion why not match him against a Cub Scout Leader just for a bit of fun? The team scores a point for each victory and the blindfold Cub Scout is changed.

(83) HANDBALL RELAY.

EQUIPMENT REQUIRED—Four balls and four chairs.

The Sixes are lined up in relay formation (Indian file) at one end of the room and at the opposite end of the room a chair is placed opposite each Six and two metres (six feet) from the wall. A ball is given to each Six and at the command to begin the Sixers pat the balls along the floor using one hand, twice around their respective chairs and twice through the chair legs, then back to their team, setting off player number two and so on. The first team to complete the course are declared the winners.

(84) ELIMINATE.

EQUIPMENT REQUIRED—A plastic bottle and a beanbag.

Akela stands at one end of the room with a beanbag or article of similar type, e.g. a knotted cloth, at his feet. The Cub Scouts form a circle in the centre of the room and a Cub Scout Leader spins a bottle in the centre of the circle. When the bottle comes to rest the Cub Scout that the neck of the bottle is pointing to becomes 'He' and must run to Akela and pick up the beanbag. Once holding the beanbag he is not allowed to move his feet, but may attempt to hit some other Cub Scout with it. If unsuccessful he must run to regain the beanbag and so on. When he is successful the Cub Scout who has been struck becomes a catcher too and the two may pass the beanbag between themselves to facilitate an easier throw and so on until only one Cub Scout is free, who is declared the winner. It helps if the catchers can be easily identified and to help with this they should play the game with their caps on.

(85) CONKERS PASS.

EQUIPMENT REQUIRED—Two 'conkers' made from ladies' stockings with a ball fastened at the end of one of the legs, or a knotted scarf. Two benches or chairs. Two blindfolds and a watch.

The two benches or chairs are placed on an imaginary centre line dividing the room into two halves about one metre (three feet) apart. The gap between them represents a pass between the two halves of the room. Two Cub Scouts are chosen and blindfolded. One takes up position standing by the pass on one of the benches, the other takes up position in the same half of the room as the rest of the Cub Scouts. Akela sets a time limit, for example one minute and the game is ready to begin, The object is for the two blindfolded Cub Scouts to capture by 'conking' as many Cub Scouts as possible before the time limit expires. The rest of the Cub Scouts must attempt to reach the safety of the other side of the pass. After the time limit expires points are awarded as follows. Plus two for every Cub Scout 'conked', plus one for every Cub Scout who has failed to negotiate the pass. Cub Scouts caught must sit on the bench and not interfere with the game. Then change those blindfolded.

(86) ONE TWO THREE FIRE.

EQUIPMENT REQUIRED—A piece of paper, a pen or pencil, a ruler, four beanbags, a piece of chalk.

Akela constructs a matrix labelled A, B, C, 1, 2, 3, etc., and as in the diagram letters representing the following ships are written in, any order being chosen.

	1	2	3	4	5	6	7
A	S	D	M	D	S	M	D
B	C	D	A	M	C	D	D
C	S	S	S	D	M	X	S
D	M	D	B	M	S	C	B
E	C	S	M	D	D	S	S

1 Aircraft Carrier	...	A	...	100 points
2 Battleships	...	B	...	50 points
4 Cruisers	...	C	...	30 points
10 Destroyers	...	D	...	20 points
10 Submarines	...	S	...	20 points
8 Minesweepers	...	M	...	10 points

The Sixes line up in Indian file at one end of the room and each Sixer is given a beanbag or similar object. At a distance of approximately five metres (sixteen feet) from each Six a circular target is drawn on the floor approximately one metre (three feet) wide.

The game begins and the Sixers throw their beanbags, attempting to land them in their target. They then run to the target and return the beanbag to the second team member and so on. Each time the beanbag lands inside the target the team call out first 'One', then 'Two' and finally 'Three'. When three is reached they shout 'Fire' and everyone must stop playing whilst the successful team fire a shell on to Akela's matrix. They do this by giving two co-ordinates, for example, C, 6. Akela puts a cross in that square and the team score the value of the ship sunk. The game then restarts and so on. Akela should set a time limit and the total scores of the Sixes after this has expired will denote the winner. If any Six is unfortunate enough to fire into a square already used, they simply do not score for that shot.

(87) INGENUITY SCAVENGER HUNT.

EQUIPMENT REQUIRED—Four pencils, four pieces of paper.

Akela selects a letter of the alphabet and sets a time limit. The Cub Scouts must collect and list as many things in the room as possible beginning with the chosen letter. Ingenuity should be encouraged, for example if the letter was 'E', ear, earlobe, or even Ernest, if there was such a member, could be placed on the list. The Six with the longest list are the winners.

(88) RUNNING SCORE.

EQUIPMENT REQUIRED—Two plastic footballs, chalk and a watch.

The room is marked out with chalk as in the diagram.

A2	B3	A1	B1	A3	B2

NO MANS LAND   NO MANS LAND

2M 6Ft   2M 6Ft   2M 6Ft   2M 6Ft

The Cub Scouts are divided into two teams, A and B. These take up positions in areas A1 and B2 respectively. One member from team A leaves his team and takes up position in area A2; a second member takes up position in 'no man's land', area A3. Similarly a member of team B takes up position in area B2 and one in B3. The object of the game is for the members of each team to attempt to pass and catch the ball across the area of 'no man's land' five times in succession without the ball being dropped, the first team to achieve this being declared the winners. The member of the other team occupying 'no man's land' must attempt to block and interfere with the passage of the ball, thus forcing the catchers to make mistakes. Have a Cub Scout Leader counting the number of consecutive passes at both ends of the room.

(89) BREAKAWAY.

EQUIPMENT REQUIRED—A piece of chalk.

This is a game to be played in the dark. A circle is drawn in the centre of the room denoting a safe area. One Six is chosen and these go outside the room with a Cub Scout Leader. The rest of the Cub Scouts choose individual or group spots around the edges of the room and lean on the walls, supporting themselves with their arms, thus forming a number of arches. Akela turns off the lights and the other Six re-enter the room. They come in on all fours and maintaining contact with the wall, follow it round on all fours, keeping going in a clock-wise direction as long as the lights are off. Akela decides when to turn on the lights and this is a signal for the Six on all fours to make a dash for the centre circle. The arches of course attempt to stop them for a period of four seconds, when they are accounted as caught. If when Akela turns on the lights any of the Cub Scouts are not in contact with the wall, they miss the next turn. Then a further Six goes out and so on. The winners are those who have most members safely in the centre area.

(90) SHUNTING.

EQUIPMENT REQUIRED—Chalk, wet cloth, watch.

A Cub Scout Leader draws a cross on the floor for every Cub Scout but one to stand on. This Cub Scout is the 'Shunter' and must *gently* back into someone and push them off their cross, thus taking possession. The dispossessed Cub Scout must likewise shunt someone else off their cross and so on. Akela sets a short time limit and when this expires the Shunter thus caught falls out. The time limit should vary from about five to fifteen seconds. Each time the limit expires a new Shunter is appointed and his cross is rubbed out. The last two competitors are the winners.

(91) TAKE YOUR PICK.

EQUIPMENT REQUIRED—Two lengths of string, four wet cloths.

Some kind of a screen is erected at one end of the room. This can be anything that a Cub Scout Leader can hide behind, i.e. an upturned table would do. He is armed with the wet cloths and two lengths of string are hung over the edge of the screen. All the Cub Scouts sit at the other end of the room and Akela selects individuals to creep up on the Cub Scout Leader and pull one of the strings. If the string pulled is held by the Cub Scout Leader, he gives a roar and throws the wet cloths at the Cub Scout attempting to hit him with them before he can reach the safety of the wall. If he is hit he drop outs of the game. If the Cub Scout pulls the string that the Cub Scout Leader is not holding he is safe.

(92) HEADS AND TAILS.

EQUIPMENT REQUIRED—A piece of chalk, a coin.

A line is drawn across the centre of the room. The Cub Scouts are divided into two teams. They stand toe to toe with an opponent from the other team on either side of the centre line. Akela names one team heads and the other team tails. He tosses a coin and if it comes down heads, the team called heads must attempt to catch members of the team called tails before they can reach the safety of the end wall and vice versa (touching is not sufficient). All captured Cub Scouts drop out of the game, so the successful catchers must assist their team mates. The game ends when one team is eliminated, or count up the players after a certain time to determine the winners.

(93) ESCAPE.

EQUIPMENT REQUIRED—A piece of chalk, four bean bags or similar missiles.

A circle large enough to accommodate the whole Pack is drawn in the centre of the room. All but one member of each Six take up position inside this circle. In each Six corner a Cub Scout Leader draws a one metre (three feet) circle on the floor. The object of the game is for each Six to escape from the centre circle into their Six corner. The first ones to achieve this being the winners. However, before they are allowed to escape, the beanbag must be thrown by one member of the Six from the centre circle into the one metre circle in each Six corner. Once this is achieved the whole Six attempt to reach their corner hopping with their arms folded. The three members of the other Sixes who are not inside the circle must attempt to interfere with any escaping Six by causing them to put their feet down. If they succeed those who have put their feet down must return to the centre area and again try to escape. The interfering Cub Scouts may have both feet on the floor but can only push escaping Cub Scouts with folded arms in any attempt to make them overbalance.

(94) CREEPY CRAWLY.

EQUIPMENT REQUIRED—Any small unbreakable object.

Sixes stand in Indian file in their corners and face the centre of the room where an object is placed. At the command to begin each Six crouches down and each back member goes legs astride over his team and crouches down in front. The next back member sets off and so on, until one Six is near enough to snatch the object. This team is the winner. To ensure that the teams do not cheat by stealing extra distance, make the front Cub Scout hold the ankles of the one newly crouching down each time. The last man may stretch out to the full to snatch the object as his ankles are held.

(95) I SPY, I FLY.

EQUIPMENT REQUIRED—None.

Akela says: 'I spy with my little eye something beginning with . . . ' as in conventional 'I Spy'. Two points are awarded to the Six that guess the object, but as soon as the answer is known everyone must attempt to touch it. One point for the first to touch it, one point off for the last. If anyone fails to touch it they lose a point too. Start each Six with ten points each.

(96) SNAP AND FLAP.

EQUIPMENT REQUIRED—None.

Akela tells a story about anything, it could be Treasure Island for example. Every time he repeats the name of a character or a place, the Cub Scout who notices the repetition runs to Akela as quickly as possible, puts his hand on top of Akela's outstretched hand and calls 'Snap'. One point for each race won. The Six with most points are the winners.

(97) EXHAUSTION.

EQUIPMENT REQUIRED—A chair, two skipping ropes, two benches.

The Cub Scouts are divided into two teams and take up position in relation to the equipment as shown in the diagram.

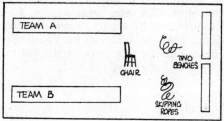

The teams are numbered from the front to the back and sit down crosslegged on the floor. Akela calls a number and the two Cub Scouts run, pick up the skipping ropes and skip ten times. Then they run to the benches and step on and off them ten times, back to the skipping ropes, skip a further ten and then race to beat their opponent to the chair to have a rest. The first one to the chair scores a point for his team. Have a Cub Scout Leader to check on the number of skips, steps, etc.

(98) CHAIN CIRCLE.

EQUIPMENT REQUIRED—A piece of chalk.

The Cub Scouts form a large circle in their Sixes and sit crosslegged on the floor. A Cub Scout Leader marks the position of each Sixer with a chalk cross on the floor. At the command to begin, the Sixer jumps up and races clockwise around the circle and back to his Six. Number two then joins on and the two complete a second circle and so on until all the Six are running for the final lap. Other teams may of course be lapped. The first Six back in their places are the winners.

(99) BLACK SPOT.

EQUIPMENT REQUIRED—A piece of paper with a black spot marked on it, a roll of transparent adhesive tape.

Everyone closes their eyes whilst Akela selects a Cub Scout and sticks a small black spot on his person somewhere by means of adhesive tape. Akela orders 'Open eyes' and the Cub Scouts must attempt to locate the black spot. If successful they tell the information to a Cub Scout Leader and are safe. The Cub Scout with the spot pretends to search for it also and the last Cub Scout to locate it drops out. The whereabouts of the spot must be told to the Cub Scout Leaders by a whisper.

NOTES

NOTES

NOTES